MW01109879

Poetry Nook

Volume 4

Frank Watson, Editor
Tiara Winter-Schorr, Editor

Plum White Press

Published by Plum White Press LLC

Copyright © 2014 by Plum White Press LLC

For information concerning reprints, email:
followingtheblueflute@gmail.com

ISBN-13:   978-1-939832-09-2
ISBN-10:   1939832098
LCCN: 2013917427
BISAC: Poetry / Anthologies

Cover design copyright © 2014 by Frank Watson

Cover image from Claude Monet's "Impression, sunrise," 1874.

Published in the United States of America

Submissions:

https://poetrynook.submittable.com/submit

Monthly Mailing List and Subscriptions:

http://www.followtheblueflute.com/p/poetry-nook-monthly.html

Also by Frank Watson

Poetry

Seas to Mulberries

Edited Volumes

The dVerse Anthology
One Hundred Leaves
Fragments

Table of Contents

Cracked Window 1
    Eusebeia Philos
I Notice 2
    Dave Read
Desperate Poet 3
    Veronica Hosking
My Mother & Her Books 4
    Stephanie Brennan
I Learn Silence 5
    Zachary Kluckman
Mother 8
    Joanna Kurowska
Standing By Water's Edge 9
    gennepher
Million Magi 10
    Subhorup Dasgupta
"A Very Serious Loss" 11
    Alexa Mergen
Untitled 12
    Rhian Williams
Web of Shadows 13
    gennepher
Dawn's Sea Mist 14
    gennepher
Tangled Roots 15
    Stephanie Brennan
She Traced 16
    Dave Read
A White Flame 17
    J.S. Petri
Once a Day 18
    Hank Archer
Hot Clouds 19
    Hank Archer
An Oceanic Telling 20
    gennepher
Spiritual Flickers 21
    Ram Krishna Singh
Susan With Black Eyes 23
    Hank Archer
Watermelons 24
    Glenna Luschei
Arctic Aria 25
    Debbie Strange

Three Apples...26
    Michael Seese
city lights 27
    Dave Read
those aren't stars 28
    Dave Read
thorns 29
    Joy McCall
Freshness..30
    Carlos Rosa
Peach Boy 31
    Daryl Muranaka
Contours 32
    Merilyn Jackson
Fog on Pan'd Glass 33
    Christine Hansen
36 Haiku from a February and March 34
    Brian Gillikin
Coma..40
    William Greenway
Toward the Light 41
    toki
The Inverted Sky is White..42
    Bauke Kamstra
Untethered 43
    Stephanie Brennan
Mid-air..44
    John Thomas Allen
Pentinence...45
    Wendy Oldenbrook
Dickens RSVP'ed 46
    Samira Noorali
Tune of a Sarrod...47
    Samira Noorali
Relishing in the Steam 48
    Samira Noorali
Six Decades..49
    Sandi Pray
Oversize Bags 50
    elle m
dead grass...51
    Dave Read
Shoveling Snow 52
    Dave Read
We Are All Summer Children 53
    Bauke Kamstra

I Sometimes Sense 54
    Bauke Kamstra
In The Day 55
    Bauke Kamstra
It Is Always Too Late To Go Back 56
    Bauke Kamstra
Willfully Blind 57
    Bauke Kamstra
On Some Wild Mornings 58
    Matsukaze
I Am Not Practical Enough 59
    Bauke Kamstra
Ode to a Half-Eaten Apple 60
    Anne Carly Abad
Old Women 61
    Doug Draime
Old New Yawk 62
    Joel Daniels
The Buffalo's Laugh 64
    Brian Miller
Interview with M. Kei 65
a fresh leaf 75
    M. Kei
this journal 76
    M. Kei
New Year's Day 77
    M. Kei
another sip of tea 78
    M. Kei
when the world of men is gone 79
    M. Kei
a bit of green 80
    M. Kei
grey ghost 81
    M. Kei
the *Sarah C. Conway* 82
    M. Kei
it's a place 83
    M. Kei
homesick 84
    M. Kei
overhead 85
    M. Kei
a line of 86
    M. Kei

wood thrush..87
    M. Kei
creeping jennies..88
    M. Kei
under the flag 89
    M. Kei
I am not Basho 90
    M. Kei
a pleasure boat 91
    M. Kei
kisses...92
    M. Kei
waking at my accustomed hour 93
    M. Kei
go deeper 94
    M. Kei

Biographies...95

Credits 102

Editors' Note

The past few months have been an incredibly rewarding experience made possible by our readers and contributors. We thank you for your support and encouragement.

We welcome you to Volume 4 of *Poetry Nook*. We have decided to simplify the experience by releasing each volume as it is ready instead of following a fixed schedule tied to the calendar.

Our feature interview this month is with poet and editor, M. Kei. We had a chance to delve into his work as a writer and the experience of heading a small journal. We hope that you appreciate the beauty of his work and the grace of his intelligence.

We have a beta version available of our site, www.poetrynook.com, but it still requires much improvement to reach its full potential. Anyone who wants to be a "beta tester" and suggest improvements, please feel free to visit the site and email one of the editors with your ideas and comments. When it is fully functional, it will have a comprehensive database of public domain and licensed poetry, a forum for new poetry and discussions, and other resources for writers.

We look forward to a full year of expanding *Poetry Nook* with your help and guidance. We welcome emails with comments and suggestions.

Best Wishes for the New Year,

Frank Watson
Email: followingtheblueflute@gmail.com
Twitter: @FollowBlueFlute

Tiara Winter-Schorr
Email: winter.schorr@gmail.com
Twitter: @twinterschorr

$100 PRIZES

FOR POETRY AND ART

Congratulations to the winners of the Volume 3 poetry and art prizes: Brad Johnson for poetry and Bobby Gutierrez for photography. Each will receive a $100 prize.

We will announce the winners for Volume 4's work in the next issue. Please note that for next issue (Volume 5) there will be only one winner and we will discontinue the prize beginning with the work in Volume 6.

Instead of prizes for one or two contributors, we will send free paperback copies of *Poetry Nook* to all contributors who use *Submittable* for their submissions and provide their mailing addresses in *Submittable* (contributors outside North America or Western Europe will need to pay a $10 international shipping fee, however, to receive a free copy).

Poetry Nook

Volume 4

Cracked Window

Every day
she stared out
through a cracked window
at the world around her,
and came to understand life
in shattered visions
and missing pieces.

Eusebeia Philos

I Notice

I notice
the neighbor
noticing me
through a crack
in his blinds
through a crack
in my blinds.

Dave Read

Desperate Poet

Dirty dishes
ignored
in the sink

Words
scrawled on paper
Housewife
smeared in ink

Veronica Hosking

My Mother & Her Books

A Tanka Sequence

I often wonder
why my mother
had so many children
no time for one or any
her nose always in a book

on a dust jacket
in my mother's library
a man and woman kiss
my fingertips
I, too young to read

very young
younger than most
I learn the words
ravenous to understand
to what lands my mother sailed

a used-book sale
my mother and I gather
unknown volumes
by the end of Chapter 1
her death comes as a shock

a cache of weapons
against forgetting
a long lyric poem
and a recording
of my mother's voice

a young girl
has her grandmother's face
she knows her
by the mirror alone
for her birthday I buy her a book

Stephanie Brennan

I Learn Silence

I learn silence from a woman
who is not afraid to raise her voice.
This makes her silence
deeper.

My mother is like the rain
lavishing the trees with kisses,
not to express her love for them
but to make their silence
deeper.

I learn to hear the world
with ears that tune to animals sounds,
small and loud, their sounds of wounding
inform my hands of their inherited danger.
I learn to keep my hands in pocket
where the effort of keeping my peace
makes my silence deeper.

From her broken lungs
the sound of whimpers permeate
the unlit corners of our house,
on wheels and cinder blocks,
she rocks and the house moves with her.
I learn to recognize

the changing tones of her
unbearable quiet, the low mewl
of her remembering the loves she lost
or walked away from, the subtle growl
that barely moves her tongue
when she thinks of her brother.
I learn to come undone

In the silence, where it will go
unnoticed by anyone. My cot
on the floor is a harbor where a broken
bodied child crashes like sinking boats

into the swelling storm of his own
unknowing heart. I learn silence
in honor of her crying.

When the world swings
its unjust fist at my missing pieces,
my chest an empty cage filled with
memories of wings and feathered
bodies, my pulse like a song
I want to dance to, full of movements
I can remember, but not commit myself
to learning, these are the only times she sings,
her anger a rising note in pitch black
like birds on telephone lines

I learn my silence makes her angry.

She does not want this for me.
Does not want my eyes to haunt my face
like blackbirds in countless church windows,
my throat to close over my words.
She would teach me to scream.

She teaches me to write poetry.
When the cancer comes it attacks her throat.
The soft palate of her mouth removed
to get at the disease. I wonder if they know
what they commit her body to,
a quiet she has spent a lifetime
learning to refuse.

The surgery makes her silence deeper.

When it rains I write a poem
about the white noise of water
pouring over glass and the comfort
it brings me to hear this little noise.
Like static it is silent, but not empty.
When I consider a world

where my mother is gone,
her pained rocking motions
that made our home a lullaby cradle
missing, I learn silence

and the animal sound
my heart makes in its
restless, un-papered cage,
makes my silence deeper.

Zachary Kluckman

Mother

Mother lies down in the grave together with her child.
She cannot tear herself from this bundle of matter.
Then she rises to live on—a sign of resurrection.
She is the first to conquer death; her love
lives on both sides of the umbilical cord.

When the child that is a question mark dies
mother already knows the answer.
Blindfolded, she goes into eternity.
If there is no eternity, she creates it

Joanna Kurowska

Standing By Water's Edge

standing by water's edge
breeze rippling her cloak
she gazed out to sea

gennepher

Million Magi

November 2, 2012
Hyderabad

Climbing dirty rough-hewn stairs at the end of a dimly lit yet busy alley I
reach road number one, bauble-shiny, filled with fresh flowers and cars
In an urban cool mannequined window I see my huddled hoodied self
And know in an instant the magic of being an anthology, the very best of.

I am the spirit of my times, anonymous and numberless, I am occupy, I
am love
Seeing the cheer of the festive season and the despairing faceless
alleyways
I am suddenly more than, more real than, more people than I ever have
been
And I hear the earth calling, the bodhisattvas of the earth calling, a
million magi.

I am revulsion and compassion, I am the frenzy of the possible, silent and
unmoving
An unwashed   child nagging at the stop light, intent that someone stops,
drops a coin,
Watching cold cars go by leaving warm trails of light in the sodium vapor
of the night
I am the face at every stoplight, the face that haunts you every time you
close your eyes.

I take a turn at Midtown Mall to head back home, where the garbage bins
overflow
The mother, the Empress, the Ram and Rahim, too old to play games
anymore
Fidgety, enduring, the you that you do not know. I am the dawn to the
darkest of nights
The divine gold, my time is now, I am the countless that has become one,
one million magi.

Subhorup Dasgupta

"A Very Serious Loss"

—independent wildlife scientist quoted in The Associated Press, February 27, 2005

At the edge of Denali
a trapper shot the alpha female.

Every day now the wolf pack travels
thirteen miles to where she fell.

They wait while her mate howls for her,
calling her with cries –

long cries thrown to steel skies
beyond the buffer zone.

Alexa Mergen

Untitled

She's silent now
so terribly so,
hands clasped together
for an infinity or so
and slowly turning to dust
is a whisper inside wood.
Those last minutes
were creaking and cracking,
stairs and sobs and more silence.

Rhian Williams

Web of Shadows

webs of shadows
softly spun
I wander empty rooms

gennepher

Dawn's Sea Mist

dawn's sea mists
shape shifting
into thoughts of you

gennepher

Tangled Roots

her limbs
the tangled roots of a mangrove
he, drowning in a great
limpid pool
of a saxophone solo

Stephanie Brennan

She Traced

She traced
the lines of
my palm
seeking herself in
my future.

Dave Read

A White Flame

A white flame crossing the street.
A window pane with snow and sleet.
Cracks on the back of everything.
Go far. Make broken things sing.

J.S. Petri

Once a Day

once a day
I let myself
think of you;
sunrise over
freshly fallen snow

Hank Archer

Hot Clouds

bed sheets tumble
out the dryer door
like hot clouds;
upstairs the thunder
of her accusations

Hank Archer

An Oceanic Telling

an oceanic telling
her silken soul
adrift

gennepher

Spiritual Flickers

A Tanka Sequence

Plodding away at
season's conspiracies
life has proved untrue
with God an empty word
and prayers helpless cries

I wish I could live
nature's rhythm free from
bondage of clock-time
rituals of work and sleep
expanding haiku present

on the prayer mat
the hands raised in *vajrasan*
couldn't contact God—
the prayer was too long and
the winter night still longer

the mind creates
withdrawn to its own pleasures
a green thought
behind the banyan tree
behind the flickering lust

I can't know her
from the body, skin or curve:
the perfume cheats
like the sacred hymns chanted
in hope, and there's no answer

unknowable
the soul's pursuit hidden
by its own works:
the spirit's thirst, the strife
the restless silence, too much

unable to see
beyond the nose he says
he meditates
and sees visions of Buddha
weeping for us

the mirror swallowed
my footprints on the shore
I couldn't blame the waves
the geese kept flying over the head
the shadows kept moving afar

the lane to temple
through foul drain, dust and mud:
black back of Saturn
in a locked enclosure
a harassed devotee

not much fun—
cold night, asthmatic cough
and lonely Christmas:
no quiet place within
no fresh start for the New Year

Ram Krishna Singh

Susan With Black Eyes

she doesn't have
much money of her own;
but paints
each afternoon
a rich and salted gold

Hank Archer

Watermelons

Now you watermelons
when thieves come
pretend that you are frogs
—Basho

While our boys fought in France, braceros came North to work
the fields. When mother heard they had only a cot
she took sheets and blankets to their camp.

A man she knew pulled his wagon along our street.
"Sandías, sandías," he called.   Mother spoke
to him in Spanish. One oblong watermelon looked like a submarine.

We could see U-boats plowing up the Missouri. Men built
a tower in my Iowa neighborhood to spot the zeros from Japan.
My father was the air-raid warden and climbed the tower

when the sirens blew. We lay scared in bed until he called,
"All clear, all clear," so we could turn on the light.

"El corazón," the bracero said and plunged his machete deep
into the heart of the submarine melon. He speared the most delicious
dripping wedge I have ever tasted in my life

or ever will taste.
I could spit out the seeds.

"Say *gracías*," said mother and gave him the quarter he asked
for the melon.

Later when I moved my own family to Albuquerque, their neighborhood
was different from mine: Vietnam protests in the street. Our first night
someone stole Erich's bike.

Sunset, we drove into the red, red heart of the Sandia Mountains.
No watermelons in Sandia Pueblo. "Green reed place" was their ancient
name, a good thing in the desert. We bought watermelon
from Safeway.

Glenna Luschei

Arctic Aria

a tanka set

on the tundra
a caribou river
surging past
my inukshuk arms
carrying the midnight sun

beluga ghosts
undulate beside our boat
sea canaries
and whalebone harps
singing the horizon

seeing
with my snow eyes
opening into
negative spaces between
the ptarmigan and polar bear

blue glacier
calving into the narrows
a bloodless birth
our letting go of progeny
that too soon drift away

aurora
lithesome spirit walker
shimmering
above the taiga
rainbow ribbons in her hair

Debbie Strange

Three Apples

in the garden of eden
three apples lay
untouched
waiting for another
fall

Michael Seese

city lights

city lights
stitching
night's fabric

Dave Read

those aren't stars

those aren't
stars

but pegs
on which

the drapes
of day

are hung

after their
nightly cleaning

Dave Read

thorns

I want
brown eyes, brown hair
brown skin
how can a pale thing
hide naked in the earth?

the hedges call
old hawthorn offering
blackberries
purple-fingered, cut
I hide from the beasts

I slip
into another space
caught on
the bramble spikes
and wild rose thorns

the thorns
of the may tree
catch in my hair -
held fast, I fear nothing,
no judas, no betrayal

open the book
blood flows from every page
onto the ground -
my home-fields are bright
with scarlet poppies

Joy McCall

Freshness

words
on clotheslines rustle
I experience
a cold freshness in the lips
the wind
stirring poems in my teeth

Carlos Rosa

Peach Boy

Like the story book says,
I was an old man when you arrived.
But you didn't burst
From the pit of a giant peach
You did not tear at the succulent flesh
To break free into the world
No, you were kind
To your mother.

But in these summer waves of heat
The sticky sweet smell—
Like a sweaty peach—
Clings to your scalp, your soft hair
As you cling to me, your tiny fingers
Around mine. The other arm stretching
To hold my neck,
And I wonder, what loyal friends
Will you collect?
What ogres will you banish?
And what treasures will you find
When it is your turn to travel
Across the sea?

Daryl Muranaka

Contours

My pen traces the contours of your back
tracks of blue tattoo your skin like a map

a map of where you've been and where I want to go
from vertebrae winging down to scapulars below

floating in the wake of your brush
trailing tongue over pallor, mole and blush

along each rib -- life's little side trips --
I follow your history with searing fingertips

taut, your flesh binds sinew, vein and bone
my strokes, assaults calling forth a groan

a palpable shudder through your elongated torso
my barbed hair hedging your shoulders in *scherzo*

the cartography of your malaise
brightens under the geography of my gaze

Merilyn Jackson

Fog on Pan'd Glass

Fog on pan'd glass,
Sweat laced dreams over my skin:
Asphyxiation.

Christine Hansen

36 Haiku from a February and March

I

1

Early in the hare's year,
cracked cheeks, whitened air,
lingers Capricorn.

2

Clouds, sail-like, filled
with dawn's pale warmth, push out,
on past faded stars.

3

Lighter than breath, their
bows cut through icy peaks, those
majestic breakers.

4

Fields of silvery
statues gaze upwards, waiting
to be grass again.

5

Death, heavy as sleep,
in that teal moment before
the fire of morning.

6

Rose, lilac, indigo,
like blood, now paler, brighter,
then...Resurrection.

7

Saturn's holy goat
horn merely snowflakes fallen
on the winter sky.

8

Early birds, eyes darting
eastward, yawn, blink, blow hoar
frost into mittens.

9

Graveyards, like cities,
disturbed only by taxis,
streetlights, and drug stores.

10

Like young girls brush snow-
flakes off their coat shoulders, the
sky wipes off its stars.

11

Forests, but taller
grass, hold midnight fast under
boughs while the sky wakes.

12

Mountains, their dark hearts,
their deep bowels, where men face
forms, never sun's light.

13

They, supine giants
with thin naked hair, watch as
the last stars erode.

14

They - Caucus, Ural,
Alp, Appalachian - shoulder
the winds, weather, sky.

15

But an empty hall,
neither feather nor tuning
in its bare rafters.

16

Graveyards or cities
the same in that pale moment
after death, before life.

17

Cities, like graveyards –
dust to dust in oak paneled
coffins; Babylon.

18

Sky, earth; sword, sheath; air,
space; us, them; a great embrace –
night becoming day.

19

Sun, star ever awake,
noon, setting, stealing night, is
shortly expected.

20

Frozen dew, unbroken
but for prints of night creepers
or deliv'ry trucks.

21

Unbroken, translucent
glass, but a night hour old, it's
weeping its own death.

II

1

Crunching like thin bones
or ruptured eardrum tread through
by heavy felt boots.

2

Sing Earth, Aurora's
hymn, ancient but new. Sing that
first note of first light.

3

We roll 'round and 'round,
though Earth remains half shadow,
half day. Never more

4

than winter at poles,
summer at waist, a mix be-
tween: these, fall, and spring.

5

Dusk and dawn but a
single grey margin of our
Janus-faced home.

6

A lily, a lover
opening into the warmth
of his deep embrace.

7

Turning to him, then
away; always half his, half
the darkness'. Yet

8

some immutable point,
a drop of his blood or fire,
lies deep in her heart.

9

She receives him in
dawn's fecundity, and feels
his withdrawal at dusk.

10

Sun-like, his body
rises on top of hers; she
moon-like, gives him way.

11

Forward! Sisyphus'
rock heft through dawning Spring, long-
dayed Summer, year's dusk -

12

Cruel Corinthian's
futile task met in Winter's
night with the gods' cry:

13

Forward! Sphere circles sphere –
manacled princess dancing
round her god. Forward!

14

Liquid day, alloy
annealed by alchemist star,
quenched, tempered by night.

15

Full rotation of
human life, a year, a day –
one mold, diff'rent clay.

Brian Gillikin

Coma

It's an *m* away from comma, pause between
meanings, an *e* away from come,
petit mort. I'm lucky, always
know when it's coming, have never gone
for my lover with bloody fingernails, been
buzzed by giant wasps wearing the yellow
of medic or fireman with a stinger
of sugar. But in sleep, dreams
grow cold and clammy, my dead father
rises and shakes his head before the cock
crows—*Thou'rt too much i' the sun—*
and I find myself barely pulling back
from *the bourn of that undiscovered*
country where *what dreams may come.*
I know a hawk from a handsaw, I
say, and suddenly see one, flapping
toward me from out of the sun, talons
open, and I wake, heart hammering
to get out, and stumble to the bathroom, shaking
so hard I can hardly hold the needle, *bare*
bodkin, then stagger back to bed, spent,
and saying what I said as a child, even
knowing my parents would wake me
again, screaming, and me whispering
if I should die before I wake.

William Greenway

Toward the Light

On the journey
toward the light there are
many detours.
    In the darkness alone
    can I find what I crave.

toki

The Inverted Sky is White

The inverted sky is white
with black crows
the sprinkled stars.

Bauke Kamstra

Untethered

in the hazy twilight
a young oak
waves wildly in the wind
untethered
like a teenage daughter

Stephanie Brennan

Mid-air

In Memoriam: Harold Hart Crane
(July 21, 1899 – April 27, 1932)

Sealed violets fell from the worn
accordion on deck blue eyed man,
the dusted hat leaving
blank spaces–blanket statements,
You might say. black as the rail you
leapt from, sailor shoes damp with confetti
the threaded roses of blurry nights picked
at random, the smell
of blossomed gin unfolding
into your ripe red nose,
No one can hide in mid-air.
I am sure that a special waltz was
performed below deck,
young flappers and tight lipped
sailors wandering in secret,
slipping along the bar's rail,
the jazz all wrong, knowing it
might have been a Bridge. I am sure
the lashing marble currents of the Atlantic
carried your secrets down deep
in blinking meadows of foam.
But for that moment, Hart
when you met the sky
in a seaweed wreath
you were exposed.
The knitting women
bartenders, and seminarians all
looked up. No one can hide in
mid-air, Hart. Not even you

John Thomas Allen

Pentinence

Quiet men
in the laundramat
folding
silent apologies
to the
women who have left

Wendy Oldenbrook

Dickens RSVP'ed

dickens rsvp-ed
but only his silhouette
appeared at the door

Samira Noorali

Tune of a Sarrod

Tune of a sarrod
swims full-bodied and potent
through the scathing air

Samira Noorali

Relishing in the Steam

relishing in the steam
of a nutty latte
that drinks my soul up

Samira Noorali

Six Decades

six decades
the memory of a stream
in my pocket
the coolness of a stone
never skipped

Sandi Pray

Oversize Bags

oversize bags
she carries
the weight of
the world
under her eyes

elle m

dead grass

dead grass
like dark
whiskers
in white
beards of snow

Dave Read

Shoveling Snow

Shoveling snow
ahead of himself
he clears proof
of trespass
in advance.

Dave Read

We Are All Summer Children

We are all summer children

   winter bones
   take time to set.

Bauke Kamstra

I Sometimes Sense

I sometimes sense
that I've gotten

ahead of myself

I run
to catch up

& can't find myself.

Bauke Kamstra

In The Day

In the day
I am fire
like the sun

at night
I am quiet

not wise
but wiser.

Bauke Kamstra

It Is Always Too Late To Go Back

It is always too late to go back

   ghosts take over
   as soon as we leave.

Bauke Kamstra

Willfully Blind

Willfully blind

my dreams
take the place of sight

teaching me a substance
made

of the illusions of time.

Bauke Kamstra

On Some Wild Mornings

on some
wild mornings
i sometimes fling words
into this mosaic
of blues

Matsukaze

I Am Not Practical Enough

I am not practical enough
for ordinary life

my feet leave the ground

in my gardens
are no potatoes

only flowers grow.

Bauke Kamstra

Ode to a Half-Eaten Apple

Drop of Crimson,
who would have thought your lush curvature
would be the locus of legend,
witch's poison, deathly sleep?

You took the blame
for a world in ruin,
yet with one bite
half a worm found and you are dropped,
flesh that watered the wanting mouth
transmutes into juices spattered on rock-strewn ground.

Red taking on the color of scabs,
you lie there bruised
no better than fruits that miss harvest,
falling one by one, filling the air
with the stench of cheap wine.

Anne Carly Abad

Old Women

Old women discuss my soul,
the exact color of my hair, and
all my employment possibilities.

Egyptian sky rockets shoot dead monkeys
to Saturn; the hungry stumble down
the streets
begging for food; the valiant Mohawks
make their stand with pop guns and

Jim Beam: willing to fight and die
for what is theirs
in upper state New York. But what can I
say to the old women? They smile and
ask me for shovels
to dig up my cellar for clues
to my persistent lack of status quo.

Doug Draime

Old New Yawk

i smell like new York.

of brick and concrete. of crack smoke and homicide. if crack smoke
died, it would rest here. rotting bodies and baby mommas. red hot
sirens with words spoken in between handclaps, handicaps and
firearms. of incense tips and police sweeps. hoops with net mesh
missing halfway. 3/4 houses built by playgrounds and city parks.
local terrorism, born and bred. boars head and bread cheese rolls.
a block away from where bullets bend. better off dead what the
preacher man says, but i choose life instead. no bibles. we stack
those for use for aiming rifles.

check your coffin. what skeletons are you hiding? what crime
scenes are smoldered in the ashes and dust and debris of your
uprooted family tree? of the place you once thought you were born
to be? what happened to this hood? this town? this home. this
building. school zones scattered with unemployment food stamp
swipes and solemn faces stuck in neutral who can only go as far as
the system will take them. the system will rape them. rake them
and rate them unfit for floorboards.

it's sexy to be impoverished. to struggle. to be poor. the art world
will give you thanks and college credits. grants and scholarships.
deans will take photos with you for newsletters and website press
promotion. blogs will cover and covet you. affirmative action
supporters will rally in front of your projects with signs smelling of
sharpie and charcoal stains with words like freedom for all.

they will tell you move to places where hipsters eat cold pizza
outside of venues with funny foreign names, where bands go to die
and impress pretty drunk white girls with shaved head sides who
hold each other's purses to pee vomit, fight and fuck. they will tell
you your poorness is so pretty. it's attractive. it sells music. and
prints. and water. and you'll do things for the hood, but not in it.
away from it. because poor taste like dirt. like your mothers
glaucoma and stepfathers strokes. your fathers schizophrenia and
brothers jail sentence. and smell like new york. the one you once
carried in your back pocket. the one you only see on TV now in

biopics and photos with family you only see on holidays and in funeral homes. because that's how you remember it best. or at all. faint. like the bacon grease still saved in the fridge. for later meals.

amen and all that other sh*t.

Joel Daniels

The Buffalo's Laugh

if ever you have questions, the best person to ask
is the buffalo hidden in the back yard's tall grass

ears twitchin', he'll listen---& never raise a hoof
just chew it over//chew it over, giving you the look

that tells you what comes next
that tells you what to do

when the monkeys slip the bars
of the zoo inside of you

the trick is in the water & a healthy mud bath,
communing with the birds eating bugs from your back

& knowing
when to laugh.

Brian Miller

Interview with M. Kei

How did you first get exposed to poetry and when did you realize that it was a major passion in your life? Were you interested in poetry in general at first or was it exposure to the tanka form that ignited your interest?

I was forced to read Western literature in high school and didn't care for it. Then I was exposed to manga (Japanese comic books) and became interested in all things Japanese. In college I took a Japanese humanities course and encountered tanka. So I was 22 when I became fond of tanka. I tried to write it at the time, but failed. It was much later in life (21st century) that I returned to it.

What is it about the tanka form that attracts so much of your effort—both in your own writing and your promotion of others' work through your journal and anthologies? What do you feel is special about the tanka form that allows it to accomplish something unique compared to other short forms, such as haiku or free form micropoetry? Do you ever have poetic inspiration to express your ideas in a longer form, or do tanka sequences provide the flexibility you need in that area?

The Japanese principle of 'aware' or beautiful sadness appealed to me when I was young and still does. It was a way to experience the disappointments and perishability of the world without becoming maudlin and depressed. Tanka contains infinite possibilities, such as 'akarui', the aesthetic of brightness and noise. The five poetic phrases that make it up are uniquely strong yet flexible. This gives tanka an enduring appeal while still being able to morph into new and interesting forms. Haiku, for example, is just one of many offshoots of tanka. Haiku holds little interest for me; it lacks tanka's power to address absolutely anything.

I'm not fond of free verse because a writer can simply start writing and meander on. Tanka forces the poet to be brief and to say what he intends, which creates clarity. Tanka has evolved over 1400 years to be able to imply a great deal more than it states. This requires the reader to participate in the creation of the poem by connecting his or her own experiences with it. I sometimes write tanka prose or tanka sequences to extend an idea, but tanka in larger works are not stanzas. Tanka are autonomous. They can be pulled out of a larger work and are still coherent and meaningful. By contrast, stanzas depend on the rest of the poem for their meaning.

Tanka can be sequenced into book length works, which does not happen with free verse and other kinds of poems. An anthology of sonnets does not build into a larger whole, but is a collection of parts. I have edited several book length works; two of my collections, *January, A Tanka Diary*, and *Slow Motion : The Log of a Chesapeake Bay Skipjack*, are both diaries. They are sections of my journals, and both come out of the same year (2007). *Slow Motion* focuses on the journeys made aboard a traditional work boat, but *January* is all other subjects, such as work or hiking in the woods. Both could be characterized as 'memoirs' rather than 'collections.'

The majority of your tanka have traditional nature-connected themes, albeit with modern connections as well. For example, "grey ghost / in the winter woods, / unlike you, tree, / I will not be born again / on a spring day" or "after days / without sparrows, / suddenly a flood / of little brown birds / in the middle of the rain." We were also particularly struck by your dead deer and walk-in-the-woods poem, and your sea-inspired poems. Where do you find the inspiration for your poems? Do they just come to you as you go about your walks or your sailing, do you meditate on them after a long day, or do you ever use prompts?

I write on the spot. I pay attention to what's around me. To be a tanka poet and a sailor of traditional vessels requires paying attention, to be mindful of the world in a non-Zen way. Although it is a truism of Zen that when you try to do Zen, you aren't doing Zen. You can only do Zen when you're not doing Zen. I'm a Quaker, we believe in simplicity and awareness too, so there's nothing inherently Zen about being tuned into your own existence.

Sometimes I go looking for poems. As in, I put on my coat and hat, take a notebook and a pen, and go walking. The May poems in *January, A Tanka Diary*, about walking through the woods and finding the dead doe and fawn, those were written on the spot. I was crouching next to the bones when I wrote those poems. I have even written poems while at the wheel of a boat, but that's harder to do because you have to steer. So often I write the poems later, when I am off duty. My notebook is mottled with water stains from thrown spray or rain. Some are written from memory. Some are written from imagination.

I did experiment with writing fictional poems at one point, but they dissatisfied me. I keep my journals in the form of verse, usually tanka, but whatever small shape the poem requires. It's important to me to bear witness. I'm grateful that other locals regard *Slow Motion* as an authentic record. I hope they will also see our world truthfully depicted in my latest collection, *January*.

Do you set aside a specific writing goal each day or week, whether in hours writing or words written? How does your process for writing fiction and poetry differ?

Sometimes I feel like writing, so I write. I have the urge to write, so I do it. Other times, I noticed things and write them down. I used to live in an apartment on the first floor facing a vacant lot, so my poems were full of the birds and trees and honeysuckle seen from my window. Right now it is snowing, so there are snow poems outside my window. The poet Grunge is a friend of mine. He tells me about his spiders and gecko, so there are spider and gecko poems in my journal. (I liked insects in my poems even before meeting him.)

Fiction, non-fiction, and poetry are very different. To write fiction I need to be in a state of relaxation. I can't write fiction unless my brain is nourished and at rest. That's physically and mentally nourished. It takes a tremendous amount of energy to write the novels. Non-fiction requires a different sort of focus. I have to be detail-oriented and analytical to create my argument and support it with evidence. Poetry is something I can write at any time unless I am utterly dysfunctional. That happens because I have narcolepsy, a neurological disorder. So I have to be patient with myself. I can only do what I can do.

Editing, by contrast, is easy for me. I can edit journals and anthologies even when I when I'm unwell. Editing is a process of creative sorting. Most people don't understand editing at all. They think you just pick things and publish them. Where's the skill in that? *Fire Pearls Vols. 1* and *2* are sequenced into five seasons. They are creative narrative threads tracing through the various developments and denouements of intimate relationships.

Do you feel that having a supportive atmosphere around you is helpful for pursuing your writing career? Do your co-workers know about it? Do your friends and family encourage you in it? Or, as in some strains of Japanese poetic history, do you find an element of loneliness (sabishisa) to be essential in creating poetry?

Nobody around me takes any interest in my poetry or novels. My children are aware of it, but they won't read it. It's something I do on my own. I do have some online friends who are supportive. Twitter is an immensely supportive social environment for tanka poets. You can find me @kujakupoet there. I receive tons of email from poets, not just submissions, but comments and questions and sometimes conversations. So yes, a writer needs to cultivate an environment that furnishes his mind. Part of that is like-minded people, but it also means going out into the real world. To see different places, to choose to experience the world instead of moving blindly through it. I have written tanka in caves and college dining halls. Everything is tanka, if only we see it so.

What have you learned about writing by tackling novels after many years of successfully writing poetry?

I wrote my first novel before I succeeded in writing tanka. That was a long time ago. The thing I learned from writing the novel is that writing is a skill. It's not something you sit around waiting to be 'inspired' to do. You have to drag your butt out of the chair and do the necessary research. You have to read books to teach you how to do things that you're not good at. Then you have to practice. I spent 6–14 hours a day, 5–7 days a week on the novel until it was done. You have to make words do what you intend them to do. In that regard, novel writing and poetry writing are the same. However, the intended goal is different and the intended audience is different, so you must write in the way that addresses them. I always resent people telling me, "You're so talented!" No, I'm skilled. I worked hard for decades to be able to write what I write.

Having returned to novel writing after an extended gap, I also find that being a tanka poet has strengthened my novel writing. I can't write a plot or prepare an outline in advance; I make it up as I go along. Having written so much tanka has given me an appreciation for they way individual tanka speak for themselves, but collectively move a narrative forward. So that is applied in my novels. Likewise, the choice of the adroit detail. I also make synecdoches in fiction. An editor once attempted to edit all that out my writing, but it's a distinctive part of my style. Synecdoche is a valuable technique when you're trying to pack the maximum meaning into a small poem. I had a valuable creative writing teacher when I was a freshman in high school; he taught us poetry first. He told us that everything you learn how to do in poetry will apply to every other form of writing. He was right.

Do you plan on continuing to publish both fiction and poetry going forward? Do you see yourself leaning more towards one or the other?

I will continue both, but I am not naturally a novelist, so the novels are hard for me even when they're fun. Writers are like runners. Some runners are naturally sprinters and some are naturally marathon runners. If they try to switch events, it feels unnatural. I am naturally given to short lengths. Tanka suits my inherent strengths. By the time I finish 100K work rough draft of a novel, I'm sick of the thing. Revision is the easy part. I've written six novels in the last five years, so after *The Sea Leopard*, the current novel is done, I'm going to take a break from novel-writing.

Your *Pirates of the Narrow Seas* novels, although mainly sea adventure stories, deal with sexuality directly with a gay protagonist, yet your tanka in *January: A Tanka Diary* only rarely discuss this theme. What prompted you to explore homosexuality more directly in fiction as opposed to poetry? Was it the lack of gay protagonists in

the genre, or do you feel that the fiction form allows a fuller exploration of the theme?

Pirates of the Narrow Seas started as an attempt to entertain myself. I enjoy nautical fiction, but I was tired of the lack of gay characters. Or, when they did appear, they were very minor stereotypes whose sole purpose for existing was to get knocked down by the hero so he could prove how manly he was. I threw a book across the room in disgust, said, "I know how to write, I'll write my own story." So I invented the character of Peter Thorton and started following him around. His story makes up books 1–4 of *Pirates of the Narrow Seas*. Two additional books, *Man in the Crescent Moon* and the work in progress, *The Sea Leopard*, detail the earlier life of Captain Tangle, a major supporting character in the first four books. *Man in the Crescent Moon* is a Finalist for a Rainbow Award in the category of gay historical fiction. The winners will be announced December 9. (Book 1, *The Sallee Rovers*, also won awards.)

Tanka can address any subject, but when I am writing love poetry, I don't usually make a direct gay statement. I don't say, "I love my gay lover" in real life, I say, "I love him." If you know I'm male, then you know it's a gay poem. If you don't, then you don't. Since the reader is co-creator, they can read the genders any way that make sense to them. I have included in my biographical information that I am gay so that other LGBT tanka poets and readers will know they aren't alone.

This is true about other LGBT tanka poets I have seen as well. Gay Japanese tanka poet Ishii Tatsuhiko wrote a collection entitle *Bathhouse* that centers on his experiences at a gay bathhouse and includes overt sexuality, and Andrew Cook-Jolicoeur had a website that was dedicated to his desire to find a partner and get married, but most LGBT tanka poets are ordinary people who go about their lives in the ordinary way.

Your tanka at times mention your children and possibly hint at a heterosexual marriage in the past. Was your sexuality something you understood from an early age or did your awareness develop over time? You are currently open about your sexuality in your bio and work; was it

difficult to get to the point psychologically to be open about it? Has the current, more open, culture made a difference on a personal level?

I grew up in a time where there were no role models. Gay=child molester or gay-transvestite prostitute. I didn't relate to that, so I thought I must not be gay. I was something unique and strange. I was an oddball in all ways: gender, nerd, creative, sickly, awkward, you name it. I was it. So I was married twice, with children, and attempted to have a normal suburban life, but it never fit. I wrote my first novel then, and the main character was gay, and I realized I didn't know anything about it. So I researched it, and discovered a great many facts that helped to blow apart the stereotypes I'd been raised on. After that, I knew what I was.

Once I knew what I was, I was open about it, except where it was unsafe. That's why I use a pen name, for example. I'm employed in public education, and I dread the paranoia directed against any idea of gay men having contact with children. I also had my home and car vandalized and my children violently assaulted, so, for the sake of safety, when I moved to another town, I kept it private. It's not internalized homophobia that keeps me quiet; it's the desire to not have to spend several hundred dollars to repair my vehicle when somebody takes a baseball bat to the gay pride sticker.

Bigots hate everybody. I'm Native American on my mother's side, and my 'red pride' bumper stickers were targeted as well as my gay pride bumper stickers. Now I have nothing on my car. I also have a disability and walk with a limp, and I've been threatened with violence because of that, also. It may come as a surprise to the able-bodied, but there are bigots who specialize in beating up people with disabilities, just as there are bigots who beat up LGBT and people of color. Once you've adopted the viewpoint that you are the center of the world, then anyone who is different from you is despised.

How did you poetry career initially develop until the point where you started your own publishing firm?

Keibooks came first. I had published some poetry with journals in the Spring of 2006 when Denis M. Garrison, Michael McClintock and I planned the first *Fire Pearls*. Then Denis and Michael dropped out, and I was left holding the submissions. I decided to carry on. I'd run a small press a decade earlier, so I knew what I was doing. Print on demand and other modern technologies make small press publication much easier. So I published *Fire Pearls 1* that spring before anybody knew who I was.

We notice you've begun publishing other poets' collections, such as Joy McCall's *circling smoke, scattered bones*, under this umbrella. How would you like to develop as a publisher over the coming years?

Joy McCall is a special case. She is paraplegic and it is difficult and painful for her to sit and type, so she hired me to take her poetry and make a book of it. I can't pay royalties because I don't have the necessary accounting skills to do the financial work involved. Likewise, I don't know how to handle the tax obligation and reporting obligation when doing other people work, so I don't. Therefore, I do work-for-hire as an editor. I know how to do my own taxes to report this self-employment income, so it fits within my skill set.

On the other hand, I wouldn't have accepted the job if I didn't respect Joy's work. She's an excellent poet, and I'm pleased with *circling smoke, scattered bones*, and more importantly, so is she. I might possibly publish some other poets this way. In the meantime, Keibooks will continue publishing *Atlas Poetica : A Journal of Poetry of Place in Contemporary Tanka*, the special features and resources on the website, anthologies, and my personal work. I have already announced *Bright Stars, An Organic Tanka Anthology* that is currently accepting tanka poetry on the theme of 'akarui.' Guidelines are at:
http://atlaspoetica.org/?p=952

What qualities do you look for in the poems that you select for your journal and anthologies? What advice do you have for poets as they explore the tanka form? What do you think makes a good English tanka?

I look for poems that have something interesting to say. Other journals claim to publish only 'fine' or 'excellent' tanka, but that usually means publishing tanka that appeals to the editor's taste. I have published some tanka I don't like because I think they offered something different or interesting. I also believe that emerging poets need a place to publish where they can benefit from the response of the public to their work, so *ATPO* deliberately mixes experienced and emerging poets. It also means that experienced poets can experiment with things outside their usual work and not be typecast into publishing only the one thing they're famous for. *ATPO*, being a journal of poetry of place, looks for tanka, waka, kyoka, gogyoshi, and nonce forms that are somehow grounded in a geographical or cultural place. *ATPO* deliberately reaches out around the world for tanka and related forms. We have had issues focused on tanka in translation, and most recently, an issue focused on SE Europe.

The anthologies look for poems relevant to the theme. I don't publish generic anthologies. *Fire Pearls 1 & 2* are on the theme of love—romantic, new, old, frustrated, passionate, lonely, desperate, misunderstood, rape, domestic violence, comedy, LGBT—any aspect of love desired, gained, or lost. *Catzilla : Tanka, Kyoka and Gogyoshi about Cats* was on the theme of cats. *Bright Stars* is looking for modern tanka, urban, upbeat, bright, etc, but also dark tanka where the darkness is an active darkness, not vapid, wan darkness.

As for interested poets: read good tanka. Many are hooked on the Japanese classics in translation, but they should also read modern tanka in translation, such as Leza Lowitz's translation of *A Long Rainy Season*. They should also read excellent tanka in English, such as *Take Five : Best Contemporary Tanka, Vols. 1–4*. Or tanka in their own native language, whatever that might be. Admittedly, there is not a lot of tanka in Fante or Slovenian, but it does exist.

The following pages contain an excerpt of tanka from M. Kei's book, January: A Tanka Diary, *which we highly recommend as an example of good tanka in modern English.*

a fresh leaf

a fresh leaf
white in the winter
of a new year;
it seems a shame
to mar it with words

M. Kei

this journal

this journal,
bound in black,
a suitable coffin
for all the words
I have written

M. Kei

New Year's Day

New Year's Day
counting questions
in the lines of poems,
sometimes any syllables
are too many

M. Kei

another sip of tea

another
sip of tea,
the seagull flies
to me
through the porcelain sky

M. Kei

when the world of men is gone

when the world of men is gone,
who will scatter
the ashes of our existence,
who will place the memorial
of our dying?

M. Kei

a bit of green

a bit of green
in a sidewalk crack—
perhaps
I have already
been reincarnated

M. Kei

grey ghost

grey ghost
in the winter woods,
unlike you, tree,
I will not be born again
on a spring day

M. Kei

the *Sarah C. Conway*

the *Sarah C. Conway*
sinking through a hole
in the storm . . .
what spirits flew out
of this white world?

M. Kei

it's a place

it's a place
like no other,
full of the ghosts
of wooden boats
and dying men

M. Kei

homesick

homesick
I discover
the beauty of
a snake garden
in the April rain

M. Kei

overhead

overhead
a hawk with a snake
in its beak—
suddenly I
think of Mexico

M. Kei

a line of

a line of
lavender wisteria along
the highway;
for a moment I forget
his death

M. Kei

wood thrush

wood thrush
outside this prison window,
stay a bit longer
so that my soul
may know freedom

M. Kei

creeping jennies

creeping jennies
closed up in the cold rain,
I teach my daughter
the secret of
wild things

M. Kei

under the flag

under the flag
of heroes,
the charred ruins
of a girl
without sin

M. Kei

I am not Basho

I am not Basho,
I am that peasant
he found
digging potatoes
along the road

M. Kei

a pleasure boat

a pleasure boat
never knows the Bay
like an oysterboat does,
with winter looming
behind the horizon

M. Kei

kisses

kisses
like bruises
and the
dark shadow
of memory

M. Kei

waking at my accustomed hour

waking at
my accustomed hour,
a dream of rain
still damp on the bark
of autumn trees

M. Kei

go deeper

go deeper
into the woods
where moss
is still green
under the fallen leaves

M. Kei

Biographies

Anne Carly Abad's haiku recently received an honorable mention in the Basho Haiku Festival Tournament (Japan, 2013). Her work has appeared or will appear in the Cordite Poetry Review, Magma Poetry, Poetry Cornwall, and Strange Horizons. Find out more about her at http://the-sword-that-speaks.blogspot.com/

Hank Archer is a journalist who has only recently begun writing poetry. He takes inspiration from every aspect of the human experience. He plays in a rockabilly band, drinks coffee, and lives in Canada.

Stephanie Brennan lives among the redwoods and fog in Sonoma County, California. She's been writing fiction for many years, some of which may be found online at: People Do Things With Their Lives. Recently she has ventured into poetry having fallen in love with the tanka and haiku writers on Twitter. She started writing her own tanka under a pseudonym (@tantamount2), because who doesn't sometimes like to try on new hats?

Joel "MaG" Daniels was born in the Bronx. He writes things. He raps things. You can find his work and other musings here: thisismag.tumblr.com. You can find his music here: mrmag.bandcamp.com. Follow him on Twitter at @MrMaG254.

Subhorup Dasgupta is a Hyderabad-based writer and artist. A student of Comparative Literature from Jadavpur University, he gave up his two-decade-old corporate career to devote himself to community building and promotion of the arts. He loves tea and jazz, and hosts his own curated catalog of fine tea.

Doug Draime's newest book is *More Than The Alley* (Interior Noise Press). He lives and writes in the foothills of the Cascades.

gennepher, who lives in North Wales UK, writes haiku, tanka, micropoetry and poetry on Twitter as @gennepher She has 3 cats and a hearing dog for the deaf who is her organic hot water bottle, keeping her warm, as she sits in her potting shed writing.

Brian Gillikin is a composer, hitchhiker, and writer who works for an international education program in Tbilisi, Georgia where he lives with his exotic Georgian wife. He tweets about music and life from @briangillikin and writes about hitchhiking and the human condition at weeklyjaunt.wordpress.com.

William Greenway's tenth collection, *Everywhere at Once*, won the Poetry Book of the Year Award from the Ohio Library Association, as did his eighth collection, *Ascending Order*. Both are from the University of Akron Press Poetry Series. His newest book, *The Accidental Garden*, is forthcoming from Word Press, and his *Selected Poems* are forthcoming from FutureCycle Press. He is a Distinguished Professor of English at Youngstown State University in Ohio.

Christine Hansen is an undergraduate studying Creative Writing at Northern Michigan University. This will be her first publication. She maintains a writing blog at: http://bearlyabard.wordpress.com/ and posts Twitter haiku at https://twitter.com/automaticguru.

Veronica Hosking is a wife, mother and poet. She sold her first story, "*Carousel*", to the anthology, *Forget Me Knots…* from the Front Porch (Obadiah Press 2003). The story was reprinted in *IDEALS Mother's Day* (Guidepost 2008). Hosking's poems have been included in the anthologies, *Cosmic Brownies* and *From the Heart*. She worked as poetry editor for Mamazina magazine. Her poem, "*A Portrait of Motherhood*", appears in its spring/summer 2011 issue. More of Hosking's poems can be found on the magazine's blog - http://mamazina.wordpress.com and her own blog - http://vhosking.wordpress.com/

Merilyn Jackson regularly writes on dance for *The Philadelphia Inquirer, Broad Street Review,* national publications such as *Pointe, Dance,* and *Dance Teacher* magazines. She specializes in the arts, literature, food, travel, and Eastern European culture and politics. More than 800 of her articles have appeared in publications as diverse as *The New York Times, The Arizona Republic, Phoenix New Times, Arizona Highways, The Warsaw Voice,* and *MIT's Technology Review.*

Bauke Kamstra has been a visual artist for over thirty years, and considers this good training for poetry. He now resides in Nova Scotia, where in the early mornings he continues to listen to what the silence tells him, & translate it into poetry. His poetry has been previous published by Poetry Nook Magazine and the Vine Leaves Journal (including the "Best of Vine Leaves 2013"). You can find more of his work at on twitter by following @wyrde.

M. Kei is a tall ship sailor and award-winning poet. He is the editor-in-chief of *Take Five : Best Contemporary Tanka,* and the editor of *Atlas Poetica : A Journal of Poetry of Place in Contemporary Tanka.* His second collection of poetry, *Slow Motion : The Log of a Chesapeake Bay Skipjack,* is Recommend Reading by the Chesapeake Bay Project. He also the author of *Fire Dragon,* an Asian-themed fantasy / science fiction novel with a gay hero. He can be followed on Twitter @kujakupoet, or visit AtlasPoetica.org.

Joanna Kurowska is the author of five poetry volumes, most recently *The Wall & Beyond,* eLectio Publishing, 2012; *Inclusions* (forthcoming 2014, Cervena Barva Press), and *The Butterfly's Choice* (forthcoming 2015, Broadstone Media). Her work appeared in journals such as *Apple Valley Review, Atticus Review, Bateau, Christianity* and *Literature, International Poetry Review, Kultura* (Paris), *Off The Coast, Penwood Review, Room Magazine, Solo, Time of Singing, Tipton Poetry Journal,* and elsewhere. Kurowska holds a Ph.D. in literature; her critical works have appeared in *The Conradian (UK), Slavic and East European Journal, Religion And The Arts, Sarmatian Review, Southern Quarterly,* and elsewhere.

Glenna Luschei divides her time between the Blue Ridge and the Central Coast of California where she is an avocado rancher. She has received a National Endowment Fellowship for Poetry, a DH Lawrence residency and the Fortner Award. She was named Poet Laureate for the City and County of San Luis Obispo for the year 2000. She received three degrees and a Life Achievement Award from the University of Nebraska. She is a Nebraska Admiral.

elle M lives on the north shore of Lake Ontario. She is an artist, writes poetry, captures photographs and collects vintage postcards. She draws inspiration from long walks and wherever the wind carries her.

Joy McCall lives in Norwich, UK. She has written poetry for 60 years. Her tanka have been published in many journals. She has a book just out called 'circling smoke, scattered bones'.

Matsukaze is a classical/operatic vocalist, thespian, and minister. He began writing haiku seriously around 2005, and tanka around 2006. He was recently re-introduced to tanka in 2013 by M. Kei, editor of *Atlas Poetica, Journey of Poetry of Place in Contemporary Tanka*. He lives in Louisiana; dividing his time between there and Houston, TX.

Alexa Mergen's poems and stories appear in numerous magazines. Her articles on poetry appear in *Front Porch, HerCircle* and *Passages North*. She edits the blogs Day Poems and Yoga Stanza and leads poetry workshops with an emphasis on attending to the natural world. Her two chapbooks are"Three Weeks Before Summer" and "We Have Trees." Please visit alexamergen.com

Brian Miller is a poet from the east coast of the United States. He is a school teacher, father to two boys and married to the most wonderful wife. He is co-founder of the award winning One Stop Poetry and dVerse Poets Pub.

Daryl Muranaka currently resides in Boston, MA, and holds an MFA from Eastern Washington University. After graduating, he spent ten years of traveling from Spokane, Washington to Japan to Hawaii before settling in the Boston area. During that time he worked in the JET Program in Fukui Prefecture in Japan and has traveled to several other countries. His work has appeared in the *Clackamas Literary Review, Hawai`i Review, Bamboo Ridge, Crab Creek Review*, and in *Poetry East*.

Samira R. Noorali is an Austin-based writer who began her love affair with poetry early in life. In 2006, she earned her Bachelor's degree with a double major in Creative Writing and Psychology. A well-rounded writer, Noorali won academic awards for appellate advocacy while a Juris Doctor candidate at Pacific McGeorge School of Law and served as a Staff Writer for *ITL News*. Recently, Noorali wrote and published *A Simple Rebirth*, an anthology containing 38 illustrated poems. She has also written a play based on *A Simple Rebirth*, which will debut in Houston in Spring 2014.

Shelly Pehler-Isakson loves being in nature and sharing the beauty of nature through pictures. She is the owner of Wild Thing Photography.
Website: www.photosbywildthing.com

J.S.Petri lives in Germany writing poems and theatre plays, photographing and sculpturing.

Eusebeia Philos was born and raised in Cleveland, Ohio. Poetry and its ability to create an emotional experience from words and ideas has always fascinated him. Many of his long form poems can be found at eusebeiaphilos.blogspot.com. You can also find him sharing micropoetry on Twitter @Eusebeia_Philos. Eusebeia received his B.A. in Philosophy from Cleveland State University. He currently resides in the rolling farmlands of Northeastern Ohio.

Dave Read is a Canadian poet living in Calgary, Alberta. His work has previously appeared in Poetry Nook and on the Jar of Stars website. You can find his micro-poetry on Twitter @AsSlimAsImBeing.

Carlos Rosa, born in 1949, learning made with the clay texture, with the smell of green beans in flower, the lightness of the wind, and the rides with kites. Literature and medicine. Books published: "*Destinos de Vidro*", short stories, "*A cor e a textura de uma folha de papel em branco*", Estado de Pernambuco award, "*Una casa bien aberta*", children's literature, Pequeño editor, in press, Argentina, "*Sobre o nome dado*" and "*Histórias que o povo conta..*", Ed. Dulcinéia Catadora. The author has unpublished works which received national awards. Publisher of www.meiotom.art.br, columnist of www.pnetliteratura.pt, poems in www.germina.com.br and www.cronopios.com.br.

Michael Seese is a former journalist, but his current day job is in information security for a regional bank. Or as his son could say even at age three, "Daddy keeps people's money safe." He has published four books: *The Secret World Of Gustave Eiffel*, a historical fiction novel about the events surrounding the construction of the Eiffel Tower; *Haunting Valley*, a collection of fictional ghost stories centered around his home town; *Scrappy Business Contingency Planning*, which teaches corporate BCP professionals how to prepare for bad things; and *Scrappy Information Security*, which teaches us all how to keep the cyber-criminals away.

Ram Krishna Singh, a poet professor from India, has been writing tanka and haiku for over three decades. His published volumes include *The River Returns* (2006), *Sexless Solitude and Other Poems* (2009), *Sense and Silence: Collected Poems* (2010), and *New and Selected Poems Tanka and Haiku* (2012). His poems have been widely translated in various languages.
web: http://rksinghpoet.blogspot.in

Debbie Strange is a member of the Writers' Collective of Manitoba and the United Haiku and Tanka Society. Her writing has received awards, and has been published in print and online by numerous journals. Debbie is also a singer-songwriter and an avid photographer. Her photographs have been published, and were recently featured in an exhibition. Debbie is currently assembling a collection of haiga and tankart. She can be found on Twitter @Debbie_Strange.

toki is a poet whose works have appeared online and in print, with recent work appearing previously in Poetry Nook, as well as forthcoming in *Atlas Poetica* and The *Bamboo Hut*. toki likes listening to the music of the spheres, pondering the interstices of the universe and taking long walks in liminal spaces. toki tweets as @tokidokizenzen.

Rhian Williams is a Welsh poet who has been published in a few magazines, including *Glitter Wolf* for whom the writer is also a regular contributor and has performed poetry in a couple of showcases put together by the poetry classes run by the School Of Life Long Learning in Aberystwyth, UK. Her website is stars-burn.net and is @anxiousgeek on Twitter.

Credits

Veronica Hosking's poem, "Desperate Poet," was first published on the Narrator USA website in November 2013.

M. Kei's poems were excerpted from his book, *January: A Tanka Diary* (Keibooks, 2013)

Joanna Kurowska's "Mother" was previously published in her volume of poetry, *The Wall & Beyond* (eLectio Publishing, 2013)

Alexa Mergen's "A Very Serious Loss" was previously published in the chapbook *We Have Trees* (Swim Press, 2005)

Debbie Strange's poem, "Arctic Aria," was first published in LYNX 28:3, October 2013.

Made in the USA
Charleston, SC
06 February 2014